Teeth Should Not Be Optional

Teeth Should Not Be Optional:

Random Thoughts from an Insomniac

by Gina Nicole Brown

ISBN: 978-1-72391-635-9

Front cover author photo by Tiffany Cain

Back cover author photo by Pete Pinocci

For my fellow insomniacs

ACKNOWLEDGEMENTS

Twenty years ago, I shared an office with my then-colleague, Deirdre. I started capturing random thoughts in a notebook and we joked that I should one day publish it and call it, "that little book of random thoughts you pick up at the cash register." We became close friends and over the years, from time to time, she'd inquire about the book. Life happened, as it is wont to do so it sat gathering dust. Two years ago, I picked up my notebook again and with a few fits and starts, I added to my earlier collection of inspirations. Forever supportive, thank you Deirdre for waiting patiently and for your quick, and last minute editing assistance.

Thank you Gabrielle and Dominique for giving mommy the time to be creative and for oddly understanding my quirky quips at your young ages. I love you without end.

Much love to my late father, James, who missed this publishing by a year, but who, along with my mother, Francine, instilled in me a huge appreciation for books and art. My mother, partially disabled from a stroke two years ago, still remains my most ardent ally. Mom, I will read every preposterous witticism to you.

Rick, you have always understood my unconventional conventions. Thank you for catching my back when it falls. I adore you.

Heaps of appreciation to my brilliant writer friend, Chana. When you put pen to pad, you inspire me to keep writing. Thank you for encasing me with an unmatched wall of support.

Tiffany, I can't imagine my creative world without you in it. Many thanks to you and Pete for the photography shoots.

Steve and Christine, thank you for listening, questioning, and laughing with me.

And a special thank you to my sisters, Leslie and Heather, and all my other family and friends. In less direct ways, you have all helped with this project. I love you.

We writers are not sleeping. We're writing with closed eyes.

With time, we have less time.

Gina Nicole Brown

CONTENTS

FOREWARD

When Gina asked me to do the foreword for her book, I was flattered, honored, and grateful that I had a mouthful of teeth and realized that this was her way of subtly acknowledging that fact. It also made me think of all of the great foreword writers and forewords that were out there in the literary world and how this was my chance to win the Pulitzer Prize for excellence in foreword writing. It also gave me an opportunity to get to read Gina's masterpiece "Teeth Should Not Be Optional." You read that right - it's a masterpiece. Reading it will take you on a journey through Gina's beautiful mind, which will make you break out singing. I started singing John Legend's, "All of Me," the part where he says, "what's going on in that beautiful mind, I'm on your magical mystery ride..." You can sing whatever song you want, but just know that Gina's going to make you laugh, think, and question if you've been living life the right way. You're also going to fall in love with her and keep looking at her picture on the cover or on the back of the book. You need to know that she's out of your league and just be happy that you got a chance to go on a journey through her thoughts and musings. And remember it's a masterpiece and if you don't agree, you don't know anything about masterpieces. Trust me, I know about masterpieces because this is a masterpiece of a foreword.

Rick Younger
Actor, Comedian, and Singer

Section One

Body, Home, People and other random thoughts

My headache medicine has headache as a side effect.

Some sneezes just can't be blessed.

My iPhone autocorrects "food" to "good."

Back in the day, food was a word too.

I'm starting an extra gluten movement.

Is mahi mahi THAT good that it has to be said twice? If we want two orders, do we say "mahi mahi mahi mahi?"

The words "fine dining" on a food truck are

a slight exaggeration.

Wise cooks say "tent the turkey so it can breathe." I say if the turkey is still breathing, tenting is the least of my concerns.

My beef eats vegetarian so I don't have to.

I saw somebody purchase caviar. On purpose.

That salad stopped being a salad six layers ago.

The smell of coffee makes me so happy I want to punch somebody.

Is vine-ripened THAT much better than sit-

on-the-window-sill-ripened?

Apples are not a gift, even if you wrap a

bow around the box.

Just call it a yard sale. We know it's not an

estate sale. Our estate is a yard too.

If it's "used furniture," it can't also be

"excellent, like-new condition."

I forget I have clocks until daylight savings time.

I wish the folks who give out jars of cookie ingredients for gifts would go one step further and bake them. Then give them to me.

Spider webs are impressively indestructible.

I hired spiders to fix my broken heart.

If you have time to go to the bathroom,

you have time to respond to my text.

The packing peanuts' inventor laughs at us every time we try to find our package in a box.

Your bill is now ready. Fresh out of the oven? Then I'll wait until it cools down for a few weeks before I pay it.

Extra money is an oxymoron.

Common sense is not as common as its

name would imply, moreover, what IS

actually common isn't sense.

Social media is high-speed narcissism.

Let's pretend "it is what it is" never was.

This page intentionally left blank. It was blank, but then you ruined it with hopeful words of the blank that wasn't.

The last time I apologized, it was for

accepting someone's apology.

This conversation was going so much better

before you started talking.

I tried to like some people today. I just couldn't.

If honest answers are a problem for you,

please don't ask me questions.

Permanent markers should always ask you if

you are sure you want to write with them.

Does your real self talk as much as your

virtual self?

A noise machine that has a "meetings"

button would cure insomnia.

My stink bugs don't stink. No truth in

advertising.

When people talk to me, I imagine they are a

TV and I channel surf.

I continually search for the practical in

practical jokes.

"Funny you should ask" is never actually funny.

Sometimes I'm conflicted about which laws

to break.

Some people should only dance like nobody is watching...when nobody is watching.

There is never an end to the question why.

I'm sorry. I did not mean to seem interested in your camping trip. I will be clearer next time.

Suburban shopping centers have to be one of

the nine circles of hell.

Oh, I know the rules. I'm just not following them.

Silence needs to quietly start a revolution.

If it weren't for my plan B, I would never have a plan A.

People who send group text messages must

still have the Y2K bug.

Sometimes I refold a napkin just to show it I'm in control.

My driving music doesn't fully support stop

signs and red lights.

Section Two

More People, Weather, Car and other unrelated thoughts

Witnessing karma in action is the most

beautiful sight.

Oh Chris, Cris, Khris, and Kris - please have

a meeting and come to consensus. Thanks.

Who cares if it's half full or half empty? Just fill it up.

If they say they'll do it momentarily, rather than in a minute, it's steeped in attitude, bordering on disgust.

I received a wedding invitation via

Facebook. Can my gift also be virtual?

If you invite me to apply, it's not really an invitation.

How do you know that you used to have a

good memory if you can't remember

anything now?

If all your books are self-help books, and you keep getting more, is the help part working?

I wonder if all Dopplers are super because

I've never heard of a less than super

Doppler. Is there just one Doppler and its

universal use across news stations renders it

to super status?

The "threat" of snow? Oh snow, don't be a bully.

Meteorologists - if it feels like 19 degrees, just say it's 19 degrees. We'll never know that it's really 27 degrees.

Without friends posting on social media, I'd

never know if it was raining.

The only real conspiracy out there is the

maintenance light that has been on in my car

for over a month. But I don't fall for such

schemes.

I can't sit in the back seat of your cab and ignore you like a normal passenger if you ask me to help you with directions.

If an ambulance drives by with sirens on,

and I'm walking on the sidewalk, I still pull

over to the right.

Drivers should be able to see over the

steering wheel.

If you're driving, all spots should not be

blind spots.

I wish there was less diversity in driving

skills.

If you don't have a motor, I don't want to share the road. You share the sidewalk.

The 1950s left a message. They want you to return the fuzzy dice hanging in your car.

One day I will lose this gas tank roulette

game I play. But that day is not today.

I think mufflers were invented for a reason.

Your car should get one.

Driving behind a bicycle is the new reason

for being late.

If you don't understand the importance of making the green turn arrow, please get a bus pass.

I dusted off my bike this morning, but now I

don't want to get it dirty by riding it.

I wish I had the confidence of a shirtless

jogger without a six-pack.

When I do my errands in workout gear, I know I inch closer and closer to an actual workout.

I define balance by eating 3 chocolate chip cookies while reading about fitness boot camps.

I almost started to like watching curling. I'm

sorry.

I'm posting some serious medal-winning

winter weight.

I've never seen anybody fit wear a Fitbit.

Hitting the funny bone makes you cry -

maybe the funny part comes later.

If you are forced to hold it long enough,

going to the bathroom can be just as good as

an orgasm.

Being cocky takes balls. Therein lies my

problem.

Sometimes I run from my own shadow. I

need a smaller, less scary shadow.

I'm waiting for my hips to start lying.

Teeth should not be optional.

Sure, we all pick our toenails. Just not in an airport.

My goal in life is to only have one chin.

Floss. It's what should happen.

I have big hands for a woman my size, but

I don't have equally big feet. So my dating

life isn't special.

Is it still a beard if it takes up more than half of your face?

Perfume doesn't help everybody.

We can't wear deodorant to a mammogram.

Sadly, it's an event that could easily benefit from some.

I encourage women to use the men's restroom as my way of breaking down gender barriers.

Mid-life crises should be shared experiences.

My pimples makes me look younger.

I wonder who makes up the "essential" team

that determines "essential oils."

Section Three

Office, Even More People, Clothing and other unrelated thoughts

I'd like to do a study of studies, but then I'd have to do a study of the study of studies, and I'm just not that studious.

A one word email response should not have

a five-line signature plus three inspirational

quotes under it.

"To my knowledge..." is generally followed by no actual knowledge.

I don't need the pop-up blocker to pop-up

and tell me it's blocking pop-ups.

Lead with no, so a yes will always be a

nice surprise.

I think Peter Pan was on to something.

We don't need the term "legally adopted." If adoption wasn't legal, it would be abduction.

The people responsible for toy packaging

should be forcibly removed from society.

I'm a morning person that doesn't like

morning people.

Small talk is never small enough.

I thought stupid had its limits, but apparently

it was just getting started.

I should be able to tell if that's your mom or

your girlfriend.

If everybody but you is confused, you are

the problem.

I wish all conversations ended after 140 characters.

A disconnect exists between the people who like to hear themselves talk and those forced to listen to them.

How hard would it be for you to be

interesting?

What is this elusive dream thing people keep

thinking they're living?

Dating advice from perennially single people is like parenting advice from folks who don't even have a dog.

Dates are way more fun than date nights.

Dating is a gateway drug to marriage.

Makers of Crocs: if you stop making them in adult sizes, we'd stop seeing adults wearing them.

Your socks should not be more fascinating

than you are.

Sometimes I ask a lot from my clothes.

It's the "under" in "undershirt" that makes it

not a shirt.

Everybody should own a mirror.

I think "checking-in" at a cemetery is disrespectful to the many there who can't check-out.

Apparently "woo" does not come in

different languages.

It used to be uncommon to see a dog pushed around in a baby stroller, with a sweater on.

I miss those days.

I'm not a crow so I need the miles in how a

human could get there, not as a crow flies.

Limping cops don't invoke that safe feeling.

Being a "parenting expert" is an oxymoron.

Every day is practice. Like soccer or what

doctors do.

I don't want medical advice from a doctor

who smokes.

Some nights are made for prescription drugs. Some days are made for prescription drugs, too.

Should I be offended or flattered when you ask if I can recommend a good therapist? I'll give you a name, but just tell me how I should feel.

Elevators are most comfortable in awkward

silence.

Shutting up has its place.

Honorary degrees don't make you smarter.

A "commercial-free Monday" station that continually breaks into the music to discuss their commercial-freeness is not commercial-free.

Epic is now ordinary.

Gum chewing should be a privilege, not a right.

There is an elusive fine line that lives

between a deep hair conditioning and a

punctured scalp.

Be a box of Cheerios for Halloween, not a

sexy box of Cheerios.

Skirts should be longer than the underwear worn under them.

I always sit down to use the toilet, not

because I'm a woman, but so I can remain

open to the possibilities of what's to come.

You can't daintily bite into an apple in a business meeting.

There is no direct correlation between

wearing yoga pants and doing yoga.

"Hey, change of plans..." never changes the plan to a better plan.

To date, I have but one regret - losing immeasurable time deciphering if my waste material is of the can, bottle, plastic, or plain-trash-that-is-neither-can-nor-bottle-nor-plastic, persuasion.

Yesterday I asked myself out loud why I talk to myself out loud when I already hear it in my head before I say it. I didn't have a good answer for myself. The conversation continues.

I wonder if mesothelioma is as common as mesothelioma commercials.

"Long story short" is always "long story longer."

Vegans and people who drink a lot of water. We know. You're vegan. And you drink a lot of water.

ABOUT THE AUTHOR

GINA NICOLE BROWN requires a lot of sleep to function properly. Since she gets very little of it, she writes. She is a graduate of American University, and has an MBA in Business Economics from The George Washington University. She has spent an unforgivable amount of time working in Corporate America, and has a slight obsession with the Oxford comma. She is grounded by her two fearless daughters and lives in the Washington, DC area. As a comedian, poet, spoken word artist, and writer, she stays busy with many creative projects. Find out more on ginabrown.com.